easy chicken

Publications International, Ltd.

Microwave Cooking: Microwave ovens vary in wattage. Use the cooking times as guidelines and check for doneness before adding more time.

Preparation/Cooking Times: Preparation times are based on the approximate amount of time required to assemble the recipe before cooking, baking, chilling or serving. These times include preparation steps such as measuring, chopping and mixing. The fact that some preparations and cooking can be done simultaneously is taken into account. Preparation of optional ingredients and serving suggestions is not included.

table of contents

appetizers and snacks

szechuan chicken cucumber cups

- 1½ cups finely shredded or chopped skinless rotisserie chicken
- 1 tablespoon rice vinegar
- 1 tablespoon soy sauce
- 1½ teaspoons dark sesame oil
- 1 teaspoon grated fresh ginger
- ⅛ teaspoon red pepper flakes
- 1 large seedless cucumber (about 1 pound)
- ¼ cup chopped fresh cilantro

1. Combine chicken, vinegar, soy sauce, sesame oil, ginger and red pepper flakes in medium bowl; mix well.

2. Trim off ends of cucumber. Use fork to score all sides of cucumber lengthwise (or peel cucumber lengthwise in alternating strips). Cut cucumber crosswise into 20 (½-inch) slices. Scoop out indentation in one cut side of each slice to form cup.

3. Mound 1 tablespoon chicken mixture in each cucumber cup. Sprinkle evenly with cilantro. Cover and refrigerate until ready to serve.

makes 10 servings

thai coconut chicken meatballs

1	pound ground chicken
2	green onions, chopped
1	clove garlic, minced
2	teaspoons dark sesame oil
2	teaspoons mirin
1	teaspoon fish sauce
1	tablespoon canola oil
½	cup unsweetened canned coconut milk
¼	cup chicken broth
2	teaspoons packed brown sugar
1	teaspoon Thai red curry paste
2	teaspoons lime juice
2	tablespoons water
1	tablespoon cornstarch

Slow Cooker Directions

1. Combine chicken, green onions, garlic, sesame oil, mirin and fish sauce in large bowl. Shape into 1½-inch meatballs.

2. Heat canola oil in large skillet over medium-high heat. Add meatballs in batches; cook and stir 6 to 8 minutes or until browned on all sides. Remove to 4½-quart slow cooker. Add coconut milk, broth, brown sugar and curry paste. Cover; cook on HIGH 3½ to 4 hours. Stir in lime juice.

3. Stir water into cornstarch in small bowl until smooth. Whisk into sauce in slow cooker. Cook, uncovered, on HIGH 10 to 15 minutes or until sauce is slightly thickened.

makes 4 to 5 servings

Tip: Meatballs that are of equal size will cook at the same rate and be done at the same time. To ensure your meatballs are the same size, pat seasoned ground meat into an even rectangle and then slice into even rows and columns. Roll each portion into a smooth ball.

empanaditas

Chicken Filling (recipe follows)
Pastry for double-crust 9-inch pie
1   **egg yolk mixed with 1 teaspoon water**

1. Preheat oven to 375°F. Prepare Chicken Filling.

2. Roll out pastry, one half at a time, on floured surface to ⅛-inch thickness. Cut into 2½-inch circles. Place about 1 teaspoon Chicken Filling on each circle. Fold dough over to make half moons; seal edges with fork. Prick tops; brush with egg mixture.

3. Place on ungreased baking sheets. Bake 12 to 15 minutes or until golden brown. Serve warm.

makes about 3 dozen

chicken filling

1   **tablespoon butter**
1   **cup finely chopped onion**
2   **cups finely chopped cooked chicken**
¼   **cup canned diced mild green chiles**
1   **tablespoon capers, drained and coarsely chopped**
¼   **teaspoon salt**
1   **cup (4 ounces) shredded Monterey Jack cheese**

1. Melt butter in large skillet over medium heat. Add onion; cook and stir 3 to 5 minutes or until tender. Stir in chicken, chiles, capers and salt; cook 1 minute.

2. Remove from heat; stir in cheese.

makes about 3 cups

buffalo chicken tenders

3	tablespoons hot pepper sauce
½	teaspoon paprika
¼	teaspoon ground red pepper
1	pound chicken tenders
½	cup blue cheese dressing
¼	cup sour cream
2	tablespoons crumbled blue cheese
1	medium green or red bell pepper, cut lengthwise into ½-inch-thick slices

1. Preheat oven to 375°F. Spray 11×7-inch baking dish with nonstick cooking spray.

2. Combine hot pepper sauce, paprika and ground red pepper in small bowl; brush over chicken. Place chicken in prepared baking dish. Cover; marinate in refrigerator 30 minutes.

3. Bake 15 minutes or until chicken is no longer pink in center.

4. Meanwhile, combine blue cheese dressing, sour cream and blue cheese in small serving bowl. Serve dip with chicken and bell pepper slices.

makes 10 servings

macho chicken nachos

1	tablespoon vegetable oil
1	pound ground chicken
¾	cup water
1	packet (1.25 ounces) ORTEGA® Taco Seasoning Mix
1	can (16 ounces) ORTEGA® Refried Beans
4	cups tortilla chips
1½	cups (6 ounces) shredded Cheddar cheese
¼	cup ORTEGA® Sliced Jalapeños
1	cup ORTEGA® Salsa, any variety
¼	cup B&G® Black Olives, chopped

HEAT oil in skillet over medium-low heat. Add chicken, water and seasoning mix. Cook and stir 7 minutes or until sauce is thickened. Meanwhile, heat beans in microwave on HIGH (100% power) 2 to 3 minutes.

PREHEAT broiler. Spread tortilla chips in single layer on large baking pan. Top with small dollops of heated beans, chicken mixture, cheese and jalapeños. Broil about 3 minutes or until cheese is melted and chips begin to brown. Garnish with salsa and olives. Serve immediately.

makes 4 to 6 servings

Tip: To add even more macho to your nachos, top with dollops of sour cream, chopped tomatoes and sliced green onions.

hoisin barbecue chicken sliders

⅔ cup hoisin sauce

⅓ cup barbecue sauce

3 tablespoons quick-cooking tapioca

1 tablespoon sugar

1 tablespoon soy sauce

¼ teaspoon red pepper flakes

12 boneless skinless chicken thighs (3 to 3½ pounds total)

16 dinner rolls or Hawaiian sweet rolls, split

½ medium red onion, finely chopped

 Sliced pickles (optional)

Slow Cooker Directions

1. Combine hoisin sauce, barbecue sauce, tapioca, sugar, soy sauce and red pepper flakes in slow cooker; stir to blend. Add chicken. Cover; cook on LOW 8 to 9 hours.

2. Remove chicken to cutting board; shred with two forks. Return shredded chicken and any sauce to slow cooker; mix well.

3. Spoon ¼ cup chicken and sauce onto each bun. Serve with chopped red onion and pickles, if desired.

makes 16 sliders

stuffed mushroom caps

2	packages (8 ounces each) whole mushrooms
1	tablespoon butter
⅔	cup finely chopped cooked chicken
¼	cup grated Parmesan cheese
1	tablespoon chopped fresh basil
2	teaspoons lemon juice
⅛	teaspoon onion powder
⅛	teaspoon salt
	Pinch garlic powder
	Pinch black pepper
1	small package (3 ounces) cream cheese, softened
	Paprika

1. Preheat oven to 350°F. Spray large baking sheet with nonstick cooking spray.

2. Remove stems from mushrooms and finely chop. Arrange mushroom caps, smooth side down, on prepared baking sheet.

3. Melt butter in medium skillet over medium-high heat. Add chopped mushrooms; cook and stir 5 minutes. Add chicken, Parmesan cheese, basil, lemon juice, onion powder, salt, garlic powder and pepper; cook and stir 5 minutes. Remove from heat; stir in cream cheese.

4. Spoon chicken mixture into each mushroom cap. Bake 10 to 15 minutes or until heated through. Sprinkle with paprika.

makes about 26 stuffed mushrooms

wild wedges

Nonstick cooking spray
2   (8-inch) flour tortillas
⅓   cup shredded Cheddar cheese
⅓   cup chopped cooked chicken
1   green onion, thinly sliced
2   tablespoons mild thick and chunky salsa

Heat large nonstick skillet over medium heat. Spray one side of 1 tortilla with cooking spray; place in skillet, sprayed side down. Top evenly with cheese, chicken, green onion and salsa. Place remaining tortilla on top; spray with cooking spray. Cook 2 to 3 minutes per side or until golden brown and cheese is melted. To serve, cut into eight wedges.

makes 4 servings

buffalo chicken bites

2   tablespoons PROMISE® Buttery Spread, divided
1   pound boneless skinless chicken breasts, lightly pounded ¼-inch thick (about 2 breasts)
2   tablespoons cayenne pepper sauce
12 ribs celery, sliced into 2-inch pieces (36 pieces)
36 cherry tomatoes
½   cup WISH-BONE® Fat Free! Chunky Blue Cheese Dressing

1. Melt ½ tablespoon PROMISE® Buttery Spread in 12-inch nonstick skillet over medium heat. Cook chicken, turning once, 8 minutes or until chicken is thoroughly cooked. Cut into ¾-inch pieces and keep warm.

2. Microwave remaining 1½ tablespoons Spread with cayenne pepper sauce in medium microwave-safe bowl at HIGH 15 seconds or until melted; stir until blended. Add chicken; toss to coat.

3. Alternately thread celery, tomatoes and chicken on 36 wooden skewers. Arrange skewers on serving platter and serve with Dressing.

makes 12 servings

wild wedges

chicken nuggets with dipping sauce

     Dipping Sauce (recipe follows)
½   **cup panko bread crumbs**
½   **cup grated Parmesan cheese**
1   **package (3 ounces) ramen noodles, any flavor, finely crushed***
1   **teaspoon garlic powder**
1   **teaspoon dried basil**
½   **teaspoon salt**
¼   **teaspoon black pepper**
1   **egg, lightly beaten**
1½   **pounds boneless skinless chicken breasts, cut into 1×2½-inch strips**
½   **cup vegetable oil**

Discard seasoning packet or reserve for another use.

1. Prepare Dipping Sauce.

2. Combine panko, cheese, noodles, garlic powder, basil, salt and pepper in large bowl. Place egg in shallow bowl. Dip chicken in egg; shake off excess. Coat with panko mixture.

3. Heat oil in large skillet over medium heat. Add chicken in batches; cook 5 minutes or until cooked through, turning once. Serve with Dipping Sauce.

makes 4 servings

dipping sauce

1   **tablespoon olive oil**
1   **small onion, chopped**
2   **cloves garlic, minced**
¼   **teaspoon ground red pepper**
1   **can (about 14 ounces) fire-roasted diced tomatoes**

1. Heat oil in medium skillet. Add onion and garlic; cook and stir 3 minutes or until onion is tender and golden brown. Stir in ground red pepper. Remove skillet from heat. Add tomatoes.

2. Pour tomato mixture into food processor or blender; process until smooth. Return mixture to skillet; cook 10 minutes or until thickened and reduced to 1½ cups.

makes 1½ cups

sweet hot chicken wings

3   pounds chicken wings
¾   cup salsa
⅔   cup honey
⅓   cup soy sauce
¼   cup Dijon mustard
2   tablespoons vegetable oil
1   tablespoon grated fresh ginger
½   teaspoon grated lemon peel
½   teaspoon grated orange peel

1. Cut off and discard wing tips from chicken. Cut each wing in half at joint. Place wings in 13×9-inch baking dish.

2. Combine salsa, honey, soy sauce, mustard, oil, ginger, lemon peel and orange peel in small bowl; stir to blend. Pour over wings. Marinate, covered, in refrigerator at least 6 hours or overnight.

3. Preheat oven to 400°F. Bake 40 to 45 minutes or until wings are cooked through and browned.

makes about 34 appetizers

crispy ranch chicken bites

Nonstick cooking spray
¾   cup ranch dressing, plus additional for serving
2   cups panko bread crumbs
1   pound boneless skinless chicken breasts, cut into 1-inch cubes

1. Preheat oven to 375°F. Line baking sheet with foil; spray foil with cooking spray.

2. Place ¾ cup ranch dressing in small bowl. Spread panko in medium shallow bowl. Dip chicken in ranch dressing; shake off excess. Coat with panko. Place breaded chicken on prepared baking sheet; spray chicken with cooking spray.

3. Bake 15 to 17 minutes or until golden brown and cooked through, turning once. Serve with additional ranch dressing.

makes 4 servings

oven-baked spicy wings

2   pounds chicken wings
3   tablespoons COUNTRY CROCK® Calcium plus Vitamin D, melted
2   tablespoons red wine vinegar
1   to 2 tablespoons cayenne pepper sauce

1. Preheat oven to 450°F. Cut tips off wings (save tips for soup, if desired). Cut wings in half at joint. Arrange chicken wings in large roasting pan or broiler pan without the rack. Bake 50 minutes or until chicken is thoroughly cooked and crisp.

2. Combine remaining ingredients in large bowl. Add cooked chicken and toss to coat. Serve, if desired, with blue cheese dressing.

makes 8 servings

Note: Baking is easier and less messy than frying these classic appetizers.

crispy ranch
chicken bites

original buffalo chicken wings

       Zesty Blue Cheese Dip (recipe follows)
2½ **pounds chicken wings, split and tips discarded**
½   **cup FRANK'S® REDHOT® Original Cayenne Pepper Sauce (or to taste)**
⅓   **cup butter or margarine, melted**
       Celery sticks

PREPARE Zesty Blue Cheese Dip.

DEEP FRY* wings at 400°F 12 minutes or until crisp and no longer pink; drain.

COMBINE Frank's RedHot Sauce and butter in large bowl. Add wings to sauce; toss well to coat evenly. Serve with Zesty Blue Cheese Dip and celery.

makes 24 to 30 individual pieces

Or prepare wings using one of the cooking methods below. Add wings to sauce; toss well to coat evenly.

To Bake: Place wings in single layer on rack in foil-lined roasting pan. Bake at 425°F 1 hour or until crisp and no longer pink, turning once halfway through baking time.

To Broil: Place wings in single layer on rack in foil-lined roasting pan. Broil 6 inches from heat 15 to 20 minutes or until crisp and no longer pink, turning once halfway through cooking time.

To Grill: Place wings on oiled grid. Grill over medium heat 30 to 40 minutes or until crisp and no longer pink, turning often.

zesty blue cheese dip

½   **cup blue cheese salad dressing**
¼   **cup sour cream**
2   **teaspoons FRANK'S® REDHOT® Original Cayenne Pepper Sauce**

COMBINE all ingredients in medium serving bowl; mix well. Garnish with crumbled blue cheese, if desired.

makes ¾ cup

great grilling

sesame hoisin beer-can chicken

1	can (12 ounces) beer, divided
½	cup hoisin sauce
2	tablespoons honey
1	tablespoon soy sauce
1	teaspoon chili garlic sauce
½	teaspoon dark sesame oil
1	whole chicken (3½ to 4 pounds)

1. Prepare grill for indirect cooking. Combine 2 tablespoons beer, hoisin sauce, honey, soy sauce, chili garlic sauce and sesame oil in small bowl. Gently loosen skin of chicken over breast meat, legs and thighs. Spoon half of hoisin mixture evenly under skin and into cavity. Pour off beer until can is two-thirds full. Hold chicken upright with opening of cavity pointing down. Insert beer can into cavity.

2. Oil grill grid. Stand chicken upright on can over drip pan. Spread legs slightly to help support chicken. Cover; grill 30 minutes over medium indirect heat. Brush chicken with remaining hoisin mixture. Cover; grill 45 to 60 minutes or until chicken is cooked through (165°F). Use metal tongs to remove chicken and can to cutting board; let rest, standing up, 5 minutes. Carefully remove can and discard. Carve chicken and serve.

makes 8 to 10 servings

grilled chicken with chimichurri salsa

4   boneless skinless chicken breasts (6 ounces each)
½   cup plus 4 teaspoons olive oil, divided
    Salt and black pepper
½   cup finely chopped fresh parsley
¼   cup white wine vinegar
2   tablespoons finely chopped onion
3   cloves garlic, minced
1   fresh or canned jalapeño pepper,* finely chopped
2   teaspoons dried oregano

*Jalapeño peppers can sting and irritate the skin, so wear rubber gloves when handling peppers and do not touch your eyes.

1. Prepare grill for direct cooking.

2. Brush chicken with 4 teaspoons oil; season with salt and pepper. Place on grid over medium heat. Grill, covered, 10 to 16 minutes or until chicken cooked through, turning once.

3. For salsa, combine parsley, remaining ½ cup oil, vinegar, onion, garlic, jalapeño pepper and oregano. Season with salt and pepper. Serve over chicken.

makes 4 servings

Tip: Chimichurri salsa will taste best if eaten within 24 hours.

spicy orange chicken kabobs

2	boneless skinless chicken breasts (4 ounces each)
1	small red or green bell pepper
24	small button mushrooms
½	cup orange juice
2	tablespoons soy sauce
1	tablespoon vegetable oil
1½	teaspoons onion powder
½	teaspoon Chinese five-spice powder*

Chinese five-spice powder consists of cinnamon, cloves, fennel seed, star anise and Szechuan peppercorns. It can be found at Asian markets and in most supermarkets.

1. Cut chicken, bell pepper and mushrooms into 24 (¾-inch) square pieces. Combine chicken, bell pepper, orange juice, soy sauce, oil, onion powder and five-spice powder in large resealable food storage bag. Seal bag; turn to coat. Marinate in refrigerator 4 to 24 hours, turning frequently.

2. Soak 24 small wooden skewers or toothpicks in water 20 minutes. Prepare grill for direct cooking over medium heat. Spray grid with nonstick cooking spray.

3. Drain chicken mixture, reserving marinade. Thread 1 piece chicken, 1 piece bell pepper and 1 mushroom onto each skewer. Place on large baking pan. Brush with marinade; discard remaining marinade. Grill skewers 5 to 6 minutes or until chicken is cooked through. Serve immediately.

makes 12 servings

spicy grilled chicken

4	boneless skinless chicken breasts
2	tablespoons minced garlic
1	tablespoon salt
1	tablespoon red pepper flakes
2	teaspoons paprika
2	teaspoons black pepper

1. Prepare grill for direct cooking over medium-high heat. Lightly score each chicken breast 3 or 4 times with knife.

2. Combine garlic, salt, red pepper flakes, paprika and black pepper in small shallow bowl. Coat both sides of chicken with garlic mixture.

3. Grill chicken 8 to 10 minutes or until chicken is cooked through, turning once.

makes 4 servings

Serving Suggestion: Excellent served with rice pilaf.

chicken kabobs
with thai dipping sauce

1	pound boneless skinless chicken breasts, cut into 1-inch cubes
1	small cucumber, seeded and cut into small halves
1	cup cherry tomatoes
2	green onions, cut into 1-inch pieces
⅔	cup teriyaki baste & glaze sauce
⅓	cup FRANK'S® REDHOT® Original Cayenne Pepper Sauce
⅓	cup peanut butter
3	tablespoons frozen orange juice concentrate, undiluted
2	cloves garlic, minced

THREAD chicken, cucumber, tomatoes and onions alternately onto metal skewers; set aside.

TO PREPARE Thai Dipping Sauce, combine teriyaki baste & glaze sauce, Frank's RedHot Sauce, peanut butter, orange juice concentrate and garlic; mix well. Reserve ⅔ cup sauce for dipping.

BRUSH skewers with remaining sauce; discard. Place skewers on oiled grid. Grill over hot coals 10 minutes or until chicken is no longer pink in center. Serve skewers with reserved ⅔ cup Thai Dipping Sauce. Garnish as desired.

makes 6 servings

chipotle orange bbq drumsticks

½   cup barbecue sauce, preferably mesquite or hickory smoked
1   to 2 tablespoons minced canned chipotle peppers in adobo sauce
1   teaspoon grated orange peel
8   chicken drumsticks (7 to 8 ounces each), skin removed,* rinsed
     and patted dry
1   teaspoon ground cumin

Use paper towels to easily remove the skin.

1. Spray grill grid with nonstick cooking spray. Prepare grill for direct cooking.

2. Combine barbecue sauce, chipotle peppers and orange peel in small bowl; stir to blend. Set aside.

3. Sprinkle drumsticks evenly with cumin.

4. Grill chicken, covered, over medium-high heat 30 to 35 minutes or until cooked through (165°F), turning frequently. Baste with sauce during last 5 minutes, turning and basting until all of sauce is used.

makes 8 servings

Serving Suggestion: Serve with 4-ounce microwaved potatoes topped with sour cream and mixed greens with balsamic vinaigrette.

thai coffee chicken skewers

1¼ pounds chicken tenders, cut crosswise into ½-inch-wide strips
⅓ cup soy sauce
¼ cup strong brewed coffee
2 tablespoons plus 2 teaspoons lime juice, divided
4 cloves garlic, minced and divided
1 teaspoon grated fresh ginger
½ teaspoon sriracha or hot chili sauce, divided
8 (12-inch) bamboo skewers
¼ cup hoisin sauce
2 tablespoons creamy peanut butter
1 tablespoon tomato paste
1 teaspoon sugar
½ cup water
1 tablespoon minced ginger
4 green onions, cut into 1-inch pieces

1. Combine chicken, soy sauce, coffee, 2 tablespoons lime juice, 2 cloves minced garlic, 1 teaspoon grated ginger and ¼ teaspoon sriracha sauce in large resealable food storage bag. Seal bag; shake well to coat. Marinate chicken in refrigerator 1 to 2 hours.

2. Soak skewers in water 30 minutes. Prepare grill for direct cooking. Whisk hoisin sauce, peanut butter, tomato paste, sugar, water, remaining 2 cloves minced garlic, remaining ¼ teaspoon sriracha sauce, 1 tablespoon minced ginger and remaining 2 teaspoons lime juice in medium bowl. Set aside.

3. Remove chicken from marinade. Thread chicken strips onto skewers, alternating with green onions. Grill skewers over medium heat 6 to 8 minutes or until chicken is cooked through, turning halfway through grilling time. Serve with peanut sauce.

makes 8 skewers

southwestern pineapple and chicken

1	can (20 ounces) DOLE® Pineapple Slices
1	tablespoon lime juice
1	tablespoon vegetable oil
1½	teaspoons chili powder
½	teaspoon dried oregano leaves, crushed
1	garlic clove, finely chopped
5	boneless, skinless chicken breast halves

• Drain pineapple; reserve ½ cup juice.

• Combine reserved pineapple juice, lime juice, oil, chili, oregano and garlic in sealable plastic bag. Add chicken. Refrigerate and marinate 15 minutes.

• Grill chicken and pineapple, brushing occasionally with reserved marinade, 5 to 8 minutes on each side or until chicken is no longer pink in center and pineapple is lightly browned. Discard any remaining marinade.

makes 5 servings

Tip: For food safety reasons, do not brush the chicken and pineapple with marinade during last 5 minutes of grilling. Used marinade must be discarded or boiled.

chicken and fruit kabobs

1¾ cups honey
¾ cup lemon juice
½ cup Dijon mustard
⅓ cup chopped fresh ginger
4 pounds boneless skinless chicken breasts, cut into 1-inch pieces
6 fresh plums, pitted and quartered
4 cups fresh pineapple pieces (about half of medium pineapple)

1. Prepare grill for direct cooking. Combine honey, lemon juice, mustard and ginger in small bowl; mix well. Thread chicken onto skewers, alternating with fruit. Brush skewers generously with honey mixture.

2. Place kabobs on grill about 4 inches from heat. Grill 5 minutes on each side, brushing frequently with honey mixture. Grill 10 minutes or until chicken is cooked through, turning and brushing frequently with remaining honey mixture. (Do not brush with honey mixture during last 5 minutes of grilling.)

makes 12 servings

thai grilled chicken

4	boneless skinless chicken breasts (about 1¼ pounds)
¼	cup soy sauce
2	teaspoons minced fresh garlic
½	teaspoon red pepper flakes
2	tablespoons honey
1	tablespoon lime juice

1. Prepare grill for direct cooking over medium heat. Place chicken in shallow baking dish. Combine soy sauce, garlic and red pepper flakes in small bowl. Pour over chicken, turning to coat. Let stand 10 minutes.

2. Meanwhile, combine honey and lime juice in small bowl; stir to blend. Set aside.

3. Place chicken on grid; brush with marinade. Discard remaining marinade. Grill, covered, 5 minutes. Brush both sides of chicken with honey mixture. Grill 5 minutes or until chicken is cooked through.

makes 4 servings

Serving Suggestion: Serve with steamed white rice, Oriental vegetables and a fresh fruit salad.

great grilling

tangy maple syrup bbq drums

8   chicken drumsticks, skin removed*
¼   cup maple syrup
2   tablespoons prepared mustard
2   tablespoons soy sauce
½   teaspoon ground allspice
¼   teaspoon salt
¼   teaspoon red pepper flakes

Use paper towels to easily remove the skin.

1. Prepare grill for direct cooking over medium heat. Coat grid with nonstick cooking spray; place over grill to heat. Add chicken; cover and cook 30 minutes or until cooked through (165°F), turning every 5 minutes.

2. Mix syrup, mustard, soy sauce, allspice, salt and red pepper flakes in medium bowl.

3. Place chicken on rimmed baking pan or 13×9 baking pan, drizzle sauce evenly over all and turn several times to coat. Let stand 5 minutes, turning once.

makes 8 servings

great grilling

grilled rosemary chicken

2	tablespoons minced fresh rosemary
2	tablespoons lemon juice
2	tablespoons olive oil
2	cloves garlic, minced
¼	teaspoon salt
4	boneless skinless chicken breasts (about 1 pound)

1. Prepare grill for direct cooking over medium heat. Spray grid with nonstick cooking spray.

2. Whisk rosemary, lemon juice, oil, garlic and salt in small shallow glass dish. Add chicken; turn to coat. Cover; marinate in refrigerator 15 minutes, turning once. Remove chicken; discard marinade.

3. Grill chicken 5 to 6 minutes per side or until chicken is cooked through.

makes 4 servings

Tip: For added flavor, moisten a few sprigs of fresh rosemary and toss on the hot coals just before grilling.

super
salads

cobb salad

1 package (10 ounces) mixed salad greens *or* 8 cups romaine lettuce
6 ounces deli chicken, diced
1 large tomato, seeded and chopped
⅓ cup bacon, crisp-cooked and crumbled
1 large ripe avocado, diced
   Crumbled blue cheese
   Prepared blue cheese or Caesar salad dressing

1. Place salad greens in serving bowl. Arrange chicken, tomato, bacon and avocado in rows.

2. Sprinkle with blue cheese. Serve with dressing.

makes 4 servings

Serving Suggestion: Serve with warm French or Italian rolls.

greek-style chicken and bread salad

2   slices stale whole wheat bread
1   clove garlic, halved
1   cup diced cooked chicken breast, chilled
1   cup halved cherry or grape tomatoes
1   small cucumber, peeled and diced
¼   cup thinly sliced green onions or ¼ cup thinly sliced red onion
2½ tablespoons chicken broth
4   teaspoons lemon juice
½   teaspoon olive oil
¼   teaspoon dried oregano
⅛   teaspoon black pepper
⅛   teaspoon salt (optional)

1. Rub each bread slice with garlic. Toast or grill bread until lightly browned and crisp. Tear into bite-size pieces. Combine bread, chicken, tomatoes, cucumber and green onions in large bowl; toss gently.

2. Whisk broth, lemon juice, oil, oregano and pepper in small bowl; pour over salad. Toss gently. Season with salt, if desired.

makes 2 (1½-cup) servings

hula chicken salad with orange poppy seed dressing

½ cup prepared vinaigrette salad dressing
¼ cup FRENCH'S® Honey Dijon Mustard
1 tablespoon grated orange peel
1 tablespoon water
1 teaspoon poppy seeds
1 pound chicken tenders
1 tablespoon jerk seasoning
8 cups cut-up romaine lettuce
3 cups cut-up fruit from salad bar such as oranges, melon, strawberries and/or pineapple

COMBINE salad dressing, mustard, orange peel, water and poppy seeds; mix well. Reserve.

RUB chicken tenders with jerk seasoning. Skewer chicken and grill over medium-high heat until no longer pink, about 5 minutes per side.

ARRANGE lettuce and fruit on salad plates. Top with chicken and serve with dressing.

makes 4 servings

chicken caesar salad

¼   cup plus 1 tablespoon Caesar salad dressing, divided
6   ounces chicken tenders, cut in half lengthwise then crosswise
    Black pepper
4   cups (about 5 ounces) prepared Italian salad mix (romaine and radicchio)
½   cup croutons, divided
2   tablespoons grated Parmesan cheese

1. Heat 1 tablespoon salad dressing in large nonstick skillet. Add chicken; cook and stir over medium heat 3 to 4 minutes or until chicken is cooked through. Remove chicken from skillet. Season with pepper; let cool.

2. Combine salad mix, ¼ cup croutons, remaining ¼ cup salad dressing and Parmesan cheese in serving bowl; toss to coat. Top with chicken and remaining ¼ cup croutons.

makes 2 servings

Tip: Radicchio is the Italian name for a red-leafed variety of chicory. Young radicchio is actually green. It turns red when the weather becomes cool, resembling a very small head of red cabbage. Radicchio has a sharp, slightly bitter flavor similar to Belgian endive.

southwest chicken salad

1   cup plus 2 tablespoons ORTEGA® Taco Sauce, any variety, divided

1½   pounds boneless chicken breasts
Juice of ½ lime

3   tablespoons mayonnaise

3   tablespoons olive oil

1   teaspoon Worcestershire sauce

½   teaspoon POLANER® Chopped Garlic

1   head iceberg lettuce, chopped

1   bag (10 ounces) mixed greens

1   cup (4 ounces) shredded taco cheese blend

6   ORTEGA® Yellow Corn Taco Shells, broken into small pieces

POUR 1 cup taco sauce over chicken breasts in shallow pan. Cover; marinate 15 minutes in refrigerator. Turn chicken breasts over and marinate in refrigerator 15 minutes longer.

PREHEAT grill about 15 minutes. Place chicken breasts on grill; cook 5 minutes. Turn over; cook another 5 minutes, until chicken is cooked through. Remove from grill; squeeze lime juice over chicken breasts and slice into strips.

WHISK mayonnaise, oil, Worcestershire sauce, garlic and remaining 2 tablespoons taco sauce in small bowl (if dressing is too thick, add more olive oil). Toss dressing in large bowl with lettuce and mixed greens. Divide mixture among serving plates. Top evenly with sliced chicken. Sprinkle with cheese and broken taco shells.

makes 6 servings

warm chutney chicken salad

Olive oil cooking spray
6   ounces boneless skinless chicken breasts, cut into bite-size pieces
⅓   cup mango chutney
¼   cup water
1   tablespoon Dijon mustard
4   cups packaged mixed salad greens
1   cup chopped peeled mango or papaya
Sliced green onions (optional)

1. Spray medium skillet with cooking spray. Heat over medium-high heat. Add chicken; cook and stir 2 to 3 minutes or until cooked through. Stir in chutney, water and mustard. Cook and stir just until heated through. Cool slightly.

2. Toss salad greens and mango in large bowl. Arrange on serving plates.

3. Spoon chicken mixture onto greens. Garnish with green onions.

makes 2 servings

Tip: If you skin and debone your own chicken breasts, be sure to reserve both the bones and skin. Let these scraps collect in a resealable food storage bag in your freezer and soon you'll have enough to make flavorful homemade chicken broth.

buffalo chicken salad italiano

½ cup FRANK'S® REDHOT® Buffalo Wings Sauce
½ cup prepared Italian salad dressing
1   pound frozen chicken tenders, thawed
8   cups torn salad greens
1   cup sliced celery
1   cup crumbled gorgonzola or blue cheese

MIX Buffalo Wings Sauce and salad dressing in bowl. Pour ½ cup mixture over chicken tenders in large bowl. Cover and refrigerate 20 minutes.

COOK chicken on electric grill pan or barbecue grill for 3 to 5 minutes until no longer pink in center.

ARRANGE salad greens, celery and cheese on serving plates. Top with chicken and drizzle with salad dressing mixture.

makes 4 servings

Tip: You may substitute 1 pound boneless, skinless chicken breast halves for the chicken tenders.

chicken & pasta caesar salad

4   small boneless skinless chicken breasts
6   ounces uncooked potato gnocchi or other dried pasta
1   package (9 ounces) frozen artichoke hearts, thawed
1½ cups cherry tomatoes, quartered
¼   cup plus 2 tablespoons plain nonfat Greek yogurt
2   tablespoons mayonnaise
2   tablespoons grated Romano cheese
1   tablespoon dry sherry or red wine vinegar
1   clove garlic, minced
½   teaspoon anchovy paste
½   teaspoon Dijon mustard
½   teaspoon ground white pepper
1   small head romaine lettuce, torn into bite-size pieces
1   cup toasted bread cubes

1. Grill chicken breasts until cooked through.

2. Cook pasta according to package directions, omitting salt. Drain and rinse under cold water until pasta is cool. Combine pasta, artichoke hearts and tomatoes in large bowl.

3. Combine yogurt, mayonnaise, cheese, sherry, garlic, anchovy paste, mustard and pepper in small bowl; whisk until smooth. Add to pasta mixture; toss gently to coat.

4. Arrange lettuce on serving plates; top with pasta salad, chicken and bread cubes.

makes 4 servings

tropical curried chicken salad

⅔	cup prepared olive oil vinaigrette salad dressing
¼	cup FRENCH'S® Extra Tenderizing™ Worcestershire Sauce
¼	cup honey
2	tablespoons FRANK'S® REDHOT® Original Cayenne Pepper Sauce
2	teaspoons curry powder
2	teaspoons minced garlic
1	pound boneless skinless chicken breasts
8	cups washed and torn lettuce leaves
¼	cup coarsely chopped unsalted cashew nuts
½	cup shredded coconut, toasted

PLACE salad dressing, Worcestershire, honey, Frank's RedHot Sauce, curry and garlic in blender or food processor. Cover; process until well blended. Reserve ½ cup curry mixture for salad.

PLACE chicken in large resealable plastic food storage bag. Pour remaining curry mixture over chicken. Seal bag; marinate in refrigerator 30 minutes.

HEAT barbecue grill. Remove chicken from marinade; discard marinade. Grill chicken 10 to 15 minutes or until no longer pink in center. Arrange salad greens on serving plates. Slice chicken and arrange over greens. Sprinkle with nuts and coconut. If desired, garnish with diced red and orange bell peppers. Serve with reserved dressing.

makes 4 servings

finger-lickin' chicken salad

½   **cup diced roasted skinless chicken breast**
½   **stalk celery, cut into 1-inch pieces**
¼   **cup drained mandarin orange segments**
¼   **cup red seedless grapes**
2   **tablespoons plain yogurt**
1   **tablespoon mayonnaise**
¼   **teaspoon soy sauce**
⅛   **teaspoon pumpkin pie spice or cinnamon**

1. Toss chicken, celery, oranges and grapes in small bowl.

2. Combine yogurt, mayonnaise, soy sauce and pumpkin pie spice in another small bowl or cup.

3. Serve as dipping sauce with chicken mixture.

makes 1 serving

Variation: Thread the chicken onto wooden skewers alternately with celery, oranges and grapes.

chicken dinners

chicken cacciatore

8　ounces uncooked rigatoni or penne pasta
1　can (about 15 ounces) chunky Italian-style tomato sauce
1　cup sliced onion
1　cup sliced mushrooms
1　cup chopped green bell pepper
　　Nonstick cooking spray
4　boneless skinless chicken breasts (about 1 pound)
　　Salt and black pepper
　　Shredded mozzarella cheese (optional)

1. Cook pasta according to package directions; drain and keep warm.

2. Meanwhile, combine tomato sauce, onion, mushrooms and bell pepper in microwavable dish. Microwave on HIGH 6 to 8 minutes, stirring halfway through cooking time.

3. Spray large skillet with cooking spray; heat over medium-high heat. Add chicken; cook 3 to 4 minutes on each side or until lightly browned.

4. Add sauce mixture to skillet; season with salt and pepper. Reduce heat to medium; simmer 12 to 15 minutes. Serve over pasta. Garnish with cheese.

makes 4 servings

chicken dinners

southern buttermilk fried chicken

 2   cups all-purpose flour
1½   teaspoons celery salt
 1   teaspoon dried thyme
 ¾   teaspoon black pepper
 ½   teaspoon dried marjoram
1¾   cups buttermilk
 2   cups vegetable oil
 3   pounds chicken pieces

1. Combine flour, celery salt, thyme, pepper and marjoram in shallow bowl. Pour buttermilk into medium bowl.

2. Heat oil in heavy deep skillet over medium heat until it registers 350°F on deep-fry thermometer.

3. Dip chicken in buttermilk; shake off excess. Coat with flour mixture; shake off excess. Dip again in buttermilk and coat once more with flour mixture. Fry chicken in batches, skin side down, 10 to 12 minutes or until browned. Turn and fry 12 to 14 minutes or until cooked through (165°F). *Allow temperature of oil to return to 350°F between batches.* Drain chicken on paper towels.

makes 4 servings

Note: Carefully monitor the temperature of the vegetable oil during cooking. It should not drop below 325°F or go higher than 350°F. The chicken can also be cooked in a deep fryer following the manufacturer's directions. Never leave hot oil unattended.

spicy mesquite chicken fettuccine

8   ounces uncooked fettuccine
1   tablespoon chili powder
1   teaspoon ground cumin
1   teaspoon paprika
¼   teaspoon ground red pepper
2   teaspoons vegetable oil
1   pound mesquite marinated chicken breasts, cut into 1-inch pieces
    Lime wedges (optional)
    Fresh cilantro (optional)

1. Cook pasta according to package directions, omitting salt. Drain.

2. Meanwhile, combine chili powder, cumin, paprika and ground red pepper in small bowl.

3. Heat oil in large nonstick skillet over medium-high heat. Add chili powder mixture; cook 30 seconds, stirring constantly. Add chicken; cook and stir 5 to 6 minutes or until cooked through and lightly browned. Add pasta to skillet; cook and stir 1 to 2 minutes or until heated through. Serve with lime wedges, if desired. Garnish with cilantro.

makes 4 servings

grilled chicken tostadas

1	pound boneless skinless chicken breasts
1	teaspoon ground cumin
¼	cup plus 2 tablespoons salsa, divided
¼	cup orange juice
1	tablespoon vegetable oil, plus additional for green onions
2	cloves garlic, minced
8	green onions
1	can (16 ounces) refried beans
4	(10-inch) or 8 (6- to 7-inch) flour tortillas
2	cups sliced romaine lettuce leaves
1½	cups (6 ounces) shredded pepper jack cheese
1	ripe medium avocado, diced
1	medium tomato, seeded and coarsely chopped
	Chopped fresh cilantro (optional)
	Sour cream (optional)

1. Place chicken in single layer in shallow glass dish; sprinkle with cumin. Combine ¼ cup salsa, orange juice, 1 tablespoon oil and garlic in small bowl; pour over chicken. Cover; marinate in refrigerator at least 2 hours or up to 8 hours, stirring occasionally.

2. Prepare grill for direct cooking.

3. Drain chicken; reserve marinade. Brush green onions with additional oil. Place chicken and green onions on grid. Grill, covered, over medium-heat 5 minutes. Brush tops of chicken with half of reserved marinade; turn and brush with remaining marinade. Turn green onions. Grill, covered, 5 minutes or until chicken is cooked through and green onions are tender.

4. Meanwhile, combine beans and remaining 2 tablespoons salsa in small saucepan; cook and stir over medium heat 8 to 10 minutes or until heated through.

5. Place tortillas in single layer on grid. Grill, uncovered, 1 to 2 minutes per side or until golden brown. (If tortillas puff up, pierce with tip of knife.)

6. Remove chicken and green onions to cutting board. Slice chicken crosswise into ½-inch-wide strips. Cut green onions crosswise into 1-inch-long pieces. Spread tortillas with bean mixture; top with lettuce, chicken, green onions, cheese, avocado and tomato. Garnish with cilantro. Serve with sour cream, if desired.

makes 4 servings

chicken dinners

chicken and asparagus stir-fry

1   cup uncooked rice
2   tablespoons vegetable oil
1   pound boneless skinless chicken breasts, cut into ½-inch-wide
     strips
2   medium red bell peppers, cut into thin strips
½   pound fresh asparagus,* cut diagonally into 1-inch pieces
½   cup stir-fry sauce

Select thin stalks of asparagus.

1. Cook rice according to package directions; keep warm.

2. Meanwhile, heat oil in large skillet or wok over medium-high heat. Add chicken; cook and stir 3 to 4 minutes or until cooked through.

3. Reduce heat to medium. Add bell peppers and asparagus; cook and stir 2 minutes or until vegetables are crisp-tender.

4. Stir in sauce; cook 3 to 5 minutes or until heated through. Serve over rice.

makes 4 servings

Tip: Choose fresh-looking asparagus stalks with closed, compact tips. Open tips are a sign of over-maturity. At home, keep asparagus cold and humid. Use it quickly to enjoy the best fresh flavor and texture.

super speedy chicken on angel hair pasta

1   package (12 ounces) angel hair pasta, uncooked
1   tablespoon olive oil
3   boneless skinless chicken breasts (12 ounces), cut into 1-inch pieces
2   cups baby carrots, halved lengthwise
2   cups broccoli florets
¼   cup water
1   teaspoon instant chicken bouillon granules
1   jar (28 ounces) chunky-style pasta sauce
⅓   cup grated Parmesan cheese

1. Cook pasta according to package directions.

2. Meanwhile, heat oil in large nonstick skillet over medium heat. Add chicken; cook and stir 5 minutes. Stir in carrots, broccoli, water and chicken bouillon. Reduce heat to low; cover and cook 5 minutes or until vegetables are crisp-tender.

3. Bring pasta sauce to a boil in medium saucepan over high heat. Place pasta on plates; top with hot pasta sauce and chicken mixture. Sprinkle with cheese.

makes 6 servings

chicken parmesan stromboli

1   **pound boneless, skinless chicken breast halves**
½   **teaspoon salt**
¼   **teaspoon ground black pepper**
2   **teaspoons olive oil**
2   **cups shredded mozzarella cheese (about 8 ounces)**
1   **jar (1 pound 8 ounces) RAGÚ® Chunky Pasta Sauce, divided**
2   **tablespoons grated Parmesan cheese**
1   **tablespoon finely chopped fresh parsley**
1   **pound fresh or thawed frozen bread dough**

1. Preheat oven to 400°F. Season chicken with salt and pepper. In 12-inch skillet, heat olive oil over medium-high heat and brown chicken. Remove chicken from skillet and let cool; pull into large shreds.

2. In medium bowl, combine chicken, mozzarella cheese, ½ cup Pasta Sauce, Parmesan cheese and parsley; set aside.

3. On greased jelly-roll pan, press dough to form 12×10-inch rectangle. Arrange chicken mixture down center of dough. Cover filling bringing one long side into center, then overlap with the other long side; pinch seam to seal. Fold in ends and pinch to seal. Arrange on pan, seam-side down. Gently press in sides to form 12×4-inch loaf. Bake 35 minutes or until dough is cooked and golden. Cut stromboli into slices. Heat remaining Pasta Sauce and serve with stromboli.

makes 6 servings

chicken dinners

szechuan chicken tenders

2   tablespoons soy sauce
1   tablespoon chili sauce
1   tablespoon dry sherry
2   cloves garlic, minced
¼   teaspoon red pepper flakes
16   chicken tenders (about 1 pound)
1   tablespoon peanut oil
     Hot cooked rice (optional)

1. Combine soy sauce, chili sauce, sherry, garlic and red pepper flakes in shallow dish. Add chicken; toss to coat.

2. Heat oil in large nonstick skillet over medium heat. Add chicken; cook 3 to 5 minutes on each side or until chicken is browned and cooked through. Serve chicken over rice, if desired.

makes 4 servings

Variation: If you can take the heat, try adding a few Szechuan peppers to the dish. They are best if heated in the oven or over low heat in a small skillet for a few minutes before adding.

chicken dinners

chicken and linguine in creamy tomato sauce

1   tablespoon olive oil
1   pound boneless, skinless chicken breasts, cut into ½-inch strips
1   jar (1 pound 8 ounces) RAGÚ® Old World Style® Pasta Sauce
2   cups water
8   ounces uncooked linguine or spaghetti
½   cup whipping or heavy cream
1   tablespoon chopped fresh basil leaves *or* ½ teaspoon dried basil leaves, crushed

1. In 12-inch skillet, heat olive oil over medium heat and brown chicken. Remove chicken and set aside.

2. In same skillet, stir in Pasta Sauce and water. Bring to a boil over high heat. Stir in uncooked linguine and return to a boil. Reduce heat to low and simmer covered, stirring occasionally, 15 minutes or until linguine is tender.

3. Stir in cream and basil. Return chicken to skillet and cook 5 minutes or until chicken is thoroughly cooked.

makes 4 servings

chicken dinners

easy chicken chalupas

1   **fully cooked roasted chicken (about 2 pounds)**
8   **(8-inch) flour tortillas**
2   **cups shredded Cheddar cheese**
1   **cup mild green salsa**
1   **cup mild red salsa**

1. Preheat oven to 350°F. Lightly coat 13×9-inch baking dish with nonstick cooking spray. Shred chicken; discard skin and bones.

2. Place 2 tortillas in bottom of prepared dish, overlapping slightly. Layer tortillas with 1 cup chicken, ½ cup cheese and ¼ cup of each salsa. Repeat layers three times.

3. Bake 25 minutes or until bubbly and heated through.

makes 6 servings

Tip: Serve this easy main dish with some custom toppings on the side such as sour cream, chopped fresh cilantro, sliced black olives, sliced green onions and sliced avocado.

sandwiches and wraps

new wave chicken salad wraps

       2   cups chopped fresh spinach
       1½ cups chopped cooked chicken breast
       1   cup chopped tomatoes
       1   cup shredded carrots
       1   cup frozen corn, thawed
       2   teaspoons garlic-herb seasoning
       ¼   cup mayonnaise
      16   leaves romaine, iceberg or bibb lettuce

1. Combine spinach, chicken, tomatoes, carrots, corn, garlic-herb seasoning and mayonnaise in large bowl; mix well.

2. To serve, spoon ¼ cup chicken mixture onto each lettuce leaf; roll or fold as desired.

makes 8 servings

sandwiches and wraps

grilled chipotle chicken sandwiches

½   cup plain Greek yogurt

2   tablespoons mayonnaise

1   canned chipotle pepper in adobo sauce

2   teaspoons adobo sauce from canned chipotle pepper

⅛   teaspoon salt (optional)

1   medium lime, halved

4   boneless skinless chicken breasts (4 ounces each), flattened slightly

    Black pepper

2   slices Swiss cheese, cut in half diagonally

4   whole wheat hamburger buns, split

4   leaves romaine lettuce

4   thin slices red onion

1. Spray grid with nonstick cooking spray. Prepare grill for direct cooking.

2. Combine yogurt, mayonnaise, chipotle pepper, adobo sauce and salt, if desired, in food processor or blender; process until smooth.

3. Squeeze juice from one lime half evenly over chicken. Grill chicken over medium-high heat 10 minutes. Turn chicken; sprinkle with black pepper. Grill 10 minutes or until chicken is cooked through.

4. Move chicken to side of grill. Squeeze remaining lime half over chicken; top with cheese. Place buns on grill, cut sides down; grill until lightly toasted.

5. Arrange lettuce, chicken and onion on bottom halves of buns. Spread top halves of buns with chipotle mixture; close sandwiches.

makes 4 servings

sandwiches and wraps

timesaving thai wraps

1   package (3 ounces) chicken-flavored ramen noodles*
2   teaspoons creamy peanut butter
1½   cups packaged coleslaw mix
½   cup diced cooked chicken
8   (6-inch) flour tortillas
    Soy sauce (optional)

Discard seasoning packet or reserve for another use.

1. Cook noodles according to package directions; do not drain. Add peanut butter, 1 teaspoon at a time, stirring until melted. Stir in coleslaw mix and chicken; cover and set aside 2 minutes.

2. Spoon noodle mixture onto tortillas. Sprinkle with soy sauce, if desired. Wrap and serve immediately.

makes 8 wraps

Tip: Chicken may be contaminated with salmonella bacteria, a harmful microorganism that causes food poisoning, so careful handling is essential. Do not let the juices from uncooked poultry mingle with other foods, either in the grocery cart at the store, in the refrigerator or on the counter at home. Wash any surfaces and utensils, including your hands, that have come in contact with raw poultry, using hot, soapy water. Always cook poultry thoroughly.

sandwiches and wraps

tipsy chicken wraps

1	tablespoon dark sesame oil
1	pound ground chicken
8	ounces firm tofu, diced
½	red bell pepper, diced
3	green onions, sliced
1	tablespoon minced fresh ginger
2	cloves garlic, minced
½	cup Asian beer
⅓	cup hoisin sauce
1	teaspoon hot chili paste
½	cup chopped peanuts
2	heads Boston lettuce, separated into large leaves
	Whole fresh chives

1. Heat oil in large skillet over medium heat. Brown chicken 6 to 8 minutes, stirring to break up meat. Drain fat.

2. Add tofu, bell pepper, green onions, ginger and garlic; cook and stir 3 to 5 minutes or until green onions are softened. Add beer, hoisin sauce and chili paste; cook and stir 3 to 5 minutes or until heated through. Stir in peanuts.

3. Place spoonful of chicken mixture in center of each lettuce leaf. Roll up to enclose filling. Wrap chives arround filled leaves; tie to secure. Serve immediately.

makes about 20 wraps

glazed teriyaki chicken stir-fry sub

¼   cup FRENCH'S® Honey Dijon Mustard
2   tablespoons teriyaki sauce
1   tablespoon sucralose sugar substitute
1   tablespoon grated, peeled ginger root
1   tablespoon cider or red wine vinegar
1   tablespoon vegetable oil
1   pound boneless skinless chicken breasts, cut into thin strips
1   cup coarsely chopped red or yellow bell peppers
½   cup *each* coarsely chopped red onion and plum tomatoes
2   cups shredded Napa cabbage or romaine lettuce
4   Italian hero rolls, split (about 8 inches each)

COMBINE mustard, teriyaki sauce, sugar substitute, ginger and vinegar in small bowl; set aside.

HEAT oil in large skillet or wok over high heat. Stir-fry chicken 5 minutes until no longer pink. Add vegetables and stir-fry 2 minutes until just tender. Pour sauce mixture over stir-fry and cook 1 minute.

ARRANGE cabbage on rolls and top with equal portions of stir-fry. Close rolls. Serve warm.

makes 4 servings

sandwiches and wraps

quesadilla grande

2   (8-inch) flour tortillas

2   to 3 large fresh stemmed spinach leaves

2   to 3 slices (about 3 ounces) cooked boneless skinless chicken breast

2   tablespoons salsa

1   tablespoon chopped fresh cilantro

¼   cup (1 ounce) shredded Monterey Jack cheese

1. Place 1 tortilla in large nonstick skillet; cover tortilla with spinach leaves. Place chicken in single layer over spinach. Spoon salsa over chicken. Sprinkle with cilantro; top with cheese. Place remaining tortilla on top, pressing tortilla down slightly to adhere.

2. Cook filled tortillas over medium heat 4 to 5 minutes or until bottom tortilla is lightly browned. Holding top tortilla in place, gently turn over. Cook 4 minutes or until bottom tortilla is browned and cheese is melted. Cut in half to serve.

makes 1 serving

Variation: For a crispy finish, melt 2 teaspoons butter in the skillet. Be sure to lift the quesadilla so the butter flows into the center of the skillet. Cook 30 seconds. Turn over; cook 30 seconds. Cut into wedges to serve.

asian lettuce wraps with hoisin dipping sauce

2	tablespoons hoisin sauce
2	tablespoons pomegranate juice
½	teaspoon sugar
½	teaspoon grated orange peel
2	cups coleslaw mix or broccoli slaw mix
¾	cup frozen shelled edamame, thawed
½	cup matchstick carrots
2	tablespoons chopped fresh cilantro
½	medium jalapeño pepper,* seeded and sliced into thin strips
1½	cups cooked diced chicken
1	ounce toasted peanuts
12	Bibb lettuce leaves or romaine leaves

Jalapeño peppers can sting and irritate the skin, so wear rubber gloves when handling peppers and do not touch your eyes.

1. Combine hoisin sauce, pomegranate juice, sugar and orange peel in small bowl; set aside.

2. Combine coleslaw, edamame, carrots, cilantro and jalapeño pepper in medium bowl. Add chicken and peanuts; toss gently.

3. Arrange lettuce leaves on large plate. Spoon chicken mixture evenly on top of each lettuce leaf and drizzle with sauce.

makes 4 servings

chicken tortilla roll-ups

4	ounces cream cheese, softened
2	tablespoons mayonnaise
1	tablespoon Dijon mustard
¼	teaspoon black pepper
3	(10- or 12-inch) flour tortillas
1	cup finely chopped cooked chicken
¾	cup shredded or finely chopped carrot
¾	cup finely chopped green bell pepper
3	tablespoons chopped green onions

1. Combine cream cheese, mayonnaise, mustard and black pepper in small bowl; stir until well blended.

2. Spread cream cheese mixture evenly onto each tortilla leaving ½-inch border. Sprinkle chicken, carrot, bell pepper and green onions evenly over cream cheese leaving 1½-inch border on cream cheese mixture at one end of each tortilla.

3. Roll up each tortilla. Cut rolls into 1½-inch-thick slices.

makes about 18 slices

Tip: Wrap rolls in plastic wrap and refrigerate for several hours for easier slicing and to allow flavors to blend.

sandwiches and wraps

asian wraps

　　　Nonstick cooking spray
8　ounces boneless skinless chicken breasts or thighs, cut into ½-inch pieces
1　teaspoon minced fresh ginger
1　teaspoon minced garlic
¼　teaspoon red pepper flakes
¼　cup teriyaki sauce
4　cups (about 8 ounces) packaged coleslaw mix
½　cup sliced green onions
4　(10-inch) flour tortillas
8　teaspoons plum fruit spread

1. Spray large nonstick skillet or wok with cooking spray; heat over medium-high heat. Add chicken; cook and stir 2 minutes. Add ginger, garlic and red pepper flakes; cook and stir 2 minutes. Add teriyaki sauce; mix well.* Add coleslaw mix and green onions; cook and stir 4 minutes or until chicken is cooked through and cabbage is crisp-tender.

2. Spread each tortilla with 2 teaspoons fruit spread; evenly spoon chicken mixture down center of tortillas. Roll up to form wraps.

makes 4 servings

If sauce is too thick, add up to 2 tablespoons water to thin it.

sandwiches and wraps

chicken, bacon and vegetable sandwiches

½   cup mayonnaise
¼   teaspoon garlic powder
½   teaspoon black pepper, divided
4   ciabatta or focaccia rolls
4   boneless skinless chicken breasts (about 1¼ pounds)
1   medium zucchini, cut lengthwise into 4 slices
1   green bell pepper, cut into quarters
3   tablespoons olive oil
2   cloves garlic, minced
1½ teaspoons dried basil
½   teaspoon salt
2   Italian plum tomatoes, sliced
4   slices Provolone cheese
8   slices bacon, crisp cooked

1. Preheat broiler. Combine mayonnaise, garlic powder and ¼ teaspoon black pepper in small bowl; set aside.

2. Cut ciabatta rolls in half; set aside.

3. Combine chicken, zucchini, bell pepper, oil, garlic, basil, salt and remaining ¼ teaspoon black pepper in large resealable food storage bag. Seal bag; knead to coat. Marinate in refrigerator 2 to 4 hours.

4. Remove chicken, zucchini and bell pepper from marinade; discard marinade. Broil chicken, zucchini and bell pepper 4 inches from heat 6 to 8 minutes on each side or until chicken is cooked through. (Bell pepper and zucchini may take less time.)

5. Top bottom half of each ciabatta roll with mayonnaise mixture, zucchini, bell pepper, tomatoes, chicken, cheese and bacon. Serve open face.

makes 4 servings

sandwiches and wraps

chicken wraps

½   **pound boneless skinless chicken thighs**

½   **teaspoon Chinese five-spice powder**

½   **cup bean sprouts**

2   **tablespoons minced green onion**

2   **tablespoons sliced almonds**

2   **tablespoons soy sauce**

4   **teaspoons hoisin sauce**

1   **to 2 teaspoons chili garlic sauce***

4   **large lettuce leaves**

Chili garlic sauce is available in the Asian foods section of most large supermarkets.

1. Preheat oven to 350°F. Spray baking sheet with nonstick cooking spray.

2. Place chicken on prepared baking sheet; sprinkle with five-spice powder. Bake 20 minutes or until chicken is cooked through. Chop chicken when cool enough to handle.

3. Combine chicken, bean sprouts, green onion, almonds, soy sauce, hoisin sauce and chili garlic sauce in large bowl. Spoon chicken mixture evenly onto each lettuce leaf; roll up.

makes 4 servings

simple soups

thai noodle soup

1	package (3 ounces) ramen noodles, any flavor*
¾	pound chicken tenders, cut into ½-inch pieces
2	cans (about 14 ounces each) chicken broth
¼	cup shredded carrots
¼	cup frozen snow peas
2	tablespoons thinly sliced green onions
½	teaspoon minced garlic
¼	teaspoon ground ginger
3	tablespoons chopped fresh cilantro
½	lime, cut into 4 wedges

Discard seasoning packet or reserve for another use.

1. Break noodles into pieces. Cook noodles according to package directions. Drain; set aside.

2. Combine broth and chicken in large saucepan or Dutch oven; bring to a boil over medium heat. Cook 2 minutes.

3. Add carrots, snow peas, green onions, garlic and ginger. Reduce heat to low; simmer 3 minutes. Add cooked noodles and cilantro; cook 5 to 7 minutes or until heated through. Serve soup with lime wedges, if desired.

makes 4 servings

chicken & barley soup

1	cup thinly sliced celery
1	medium onion, coarsely chopped
1	carrot, thinly sliced
½	cup uncooked medium pearl barley
1	clove garlic, minced
1	cut-up whole chicken (about 3 pounds)
1	tablespoon olive oil
2½	cups chicken broth
1	can (about 14 ounces) diced tomatoes
¾	teaspoon salt
½	teaspoon dried basil
¼	teaspoon black pepper

Slow Cooker Directions

1. Place celery, onion, carrot, barley and garlic in slow cooker.

2. Remove and discard skin from chicken. Separate drumsticks from thighs. Trim back bone from breasts. Save wings for another use. Heat oil in large skillet over medium-high heat. Add chicken; cook 5 to 7 minutes on each side or until browned. Place in slow cooker.

3. Add broth, tomatoes, salt, basil and pepper to slow cooker. Cover; cook on LOW 7 to 8 hours or HIGH 4 hours or until chicken and barley are tender. Remove chicken to cutting board. Separate meat from bones; discard bones. Cut chicken into 1-inch pieces; stir into soup.

makes 4 servings

simple soups

spicy thai coconut soup

3 cups coarsely shredded cooked chicken (about 12 ounces)
2 cups chicken broth
1 can (15 ounces) straw mushrooms, drained
1 can (13½ ounces) light coconut milk
1 can (about 8 ounces) baby corn, drained
1 tablespoon minced fresh ginger
½ to 1 teaspoon red curry paste
2 tablespoons lime juice
¼ cup chopped fresh cilantro

Combine chicken, broth, mushrooms, coconut milk, corn, ginger and red curry paste in large saucepan. Bring to a simmer over medium heat; cook 8 to 10 minutes or until heated through. Stir in lime juice. Sprinkle with cilantro just before serving.

makes 4 (1½-cup) servings

Note: Red curry paste can be found in jars in the Asian food section of large grocery stores. Spice levels can vary among brands. Start with ½ teaspoon, then add more as desired.

simple soups

skillet chicken soup

1	teaspoon paprika
½	teaspoon salt
¼	teaspoon black pepper
¾	pound boneless skinless chicken breasts or thighs, cut into ¾-inch pieces
2	teaspoons vegetable oil
1	large onion, chopped
1	red bell pepper, cut into ½-inch pieces
3	cloves garlic, minced
3	cups chicken broth
1	can (19 ounces) cannellini beans or small white beans, rinsed and drained
3	cups sliced savoy or napa cabbage
½	cup herb-flavored croutons, slightly crushed

1. Combine paprika, salt and black pepper in medium bowl. Add chicken; toss to coat.

2. Heat oil in large, deep nonstick skillet over medium-high heat. Add chicken, onion, bell pepper and garlic; cook and stir 6 to 8 minutes or until chicken is cooked through.

3. Add broth and beans; bring to simmer. Cover and simmer 5 minutes. Stir in cabbage; cover and simmer 3 minutes or until cabbage is wilted. Ladle into six shallow bowls; top evenly with crushed croutons.

makes 6 servings

Tip: Savoy cabbage, also called curly cabbage, is round with pale green crinkled leaves. Napa cabbage is also known as Chinese cabbage and is elongated with light green stalks.

chicken barley soup

1	teaspoon olive oil
¾	cup chopped onion
¾	cup chopped carrot
¾	cup chopped celery
1	package (8 ounces) sliced mushrooms
2	cloves garlic, minced
4	cups chicken broth
1	cup chopped cooked chicken
½	cup uncooked quick-cooking barley
¼	teaspoon dried thyme
¼	teaspoon black pepper
1	whole bay leaf
	Juice of 1 lemon
	Chopped fresh parsley (optional)

1. Heat oil in Dutch oven over medium-high heat. Add onion, carrot, celery, mushrooms and garlic; cook and stir 5 minutes.

2. Add broth, chicken, barley, thyme, pepper and bay leaf. Bring to a boil; reduce heat, cover and simmer 25 minutes or until vegetables are tender.

3. Remove and discard bay leaf. Stir in lemon juice and sprinkle with parsley, if desired.

makes 8 (1-cup) servings

simple soups

chicken and wild rice soup

3   cans (about 14 ounces each) chicken broth
1   pound boneless skinless chicken breasts or thighs, cut into 1-inch pieces
2   cups water
1   cup sliced celery
1   cup diced carrots
1   package (6 ounces) converted long grain and wild rice mix with seasoning packet (not quick-cooking or instant rice)
½   cup chopped onion
½   teaspoon black pepper
2   teaspoons white vinegar (optional)
1   tablespoon dried parsley flakes

Slow Cooker Directions

1. Combine broth, chicken, water, celery, carrots, rice with seasoning packet, onion and pepper in slow cooker; mix well.

2. Cover; cook on LOW 6 to 7 hours or on HIGH 4 to 5 hours or until chicken is tender.

3. Stir in vinegar, if desired. Sprinkle with parsley.

makes 9 (1½-cup) servings

simple soups

north african chicken soup

¾	teaspoon paprika
½	teaspoon ground cumin
½	teaspoon ground allspice
½	teaspoon ground ginger
8	ounces boneless skinless chicken breast, cut into 1-inch pieces
	Olive oil cooking spray
2½	cups chicken broth
2	cups sweet potato, cut into ½-inch pieces
1	cup chopped onion
½	cup water
3	cloves garlic, minced
1	teaspoon sugar
2	cups canned whole tomatoes, undrained and cut up
	Black pepper

1. Combine paprika, cumin, allspice and ginger in small bowl. Combine 1 teaspoon spice mixture and chicken in medium bowl.

2. Spray medium saucepan with cooking spray; heat over medium-high heat. Add chicken; cook and stir 3 to 4 minutes or until chicken is cooked through. Remove from saucepan.

3. Combine broth, sweet potato, onion, water, garlic, sugar and remaining spice mixture in same saucepan; bring to a boil over high heat. Reduce heat and simmer, covered, 10 minutes or until sweet potato is tender. Stir in tomatoes and chicken; heat through. Season with pepper.

makes 4 servings

nancy's chicken noodle soup

1	can (about 48 ounces) chicken broth
4	cups water
2	boneless skinless chicken breasts, cut into 1-inch pieces
⅔	cup diced onion
⅔	cup diced celery
⅔	cup diced carrots
⅔	cup sliced mushrooms
½	cup frozen peas
4	cubes chicken bouillon
2	tablespoons butter or margarine
1	tablespoon dried parsley flakes
1	teaspoon salt
1	teaspoon ground cumin
1	teaspoon dried marjoram
1	teaspoon black pepper
2	cups cooked egg noodles

Slow Cooker Directions

1. Combine broth, water, chicken, onion, celery, carrots, mushrooms, peas, bouillon, butter, parsley, salt, cumin, marjoram and pepper in 5-quart slow cooker.

2. Cover; cook on LOW 5 to 7 hours or on HIGH 3 to 4 hours. Stir in noodles 30 minutes before serving.

makes 4 servings

shortcut chicken tortilla soup

2   cans (about 14 ounces each) chicken broth

4   boneless skinless chicken breasts (about 1 pound)

2   jars (16 ounces each) corn and black bean salsa

3   tablespoons vegetable oil

1   tablespoon taco seasoning

1   package (3 ounces) ramen noodles,* any flavor, broken into small pieces

4   ounces Monterey Jack cheese, grated

Discard seasoning packet or reserve for another use.

1. Bring broth to a simmer in large saucepan. Add chicken; cook 12 to 15 minutes or until cooked through. Remove chicken to cutting board using slotted spoon. Shred chicken with two forks.

2. Add salsa to saucepan; cook 5 minutes or until soup comes to a simmer. Return shredded chicken to saucepan; cook 5 minutes or until heated through.

3. Combine oil and taco seasoning in small bowl. Add noodles; toss to coat. Heat medium skillet over medium heat. Add noodles; cook and stir 8 to 10 minutes or until toasted. Top soup with toasted noodles and grated cheese.

makes 6 servings

Tip: Serve soup with lime wedges, chopped avocado, fresh cilantro or any of your favorites!

simple soups

chicken and wild rice soup

5	cups chicken broth, divided
½	cup uncooked wild rice, rinsed and drained
¼	cup (½ stick) butter
1	carrot, sliced
1	onion, chopped
2	stalks celery, chopped
½	(8-ounce) package mushrooms, sliced
2	tablespoons all-purpose flour
¼	teaspoon salt
¼	teaspoon white pepper
1½	cups chopped cooked chicken
¼	cup dry sherry

1. Combine 2½ cups broth and rice in medium saucepan; bring to a boil. Reduce heat to medium-low; cover and simmer 1 hour or until rice is tender. Drain; set aside.

2. Melt butter in large saucepan over medium heat. Add carrot; cook and stir 3 minutes. Add onion, celery and mushrooms; cook and stir 3 to 4 minutes or until tender. Whisk in flour, salt and white pepper until smooth.

3. Gradually stir in remaining 2½ cups broth; bring to a boil. Reduce heat to medium-low; cook and stir 2 minutes or until thickened. Stir in chicken, rice and sherry; simmer 3 minutes or until heated through.

makes 4 to 6 servings

apple and chicken soup

1	sweet potato (8 ounces)
1	tablespoon olive oil
2	stalks celery, thinly sliced
½	medium onion, chopped
1	teaspoon dried thyme
½	teaspoon dried rosemary
¼	teaspoon dried sage
¼	teaspoon ground nutmeg
2	cans (about 14 ounces each) chicken broth
1	cup apple juice
1	large McIntosh apple, peeled and chopped
⅔	cup uncooked small pasta shells
¾	pound boneless skinless chicken breasts, cut into ¼-inch strips

1. Pierce sweet potato all over with fork. Microwave on HIGH 6 minutes or until crisp-tender; let stand.

2. Heat oil in large saucepan over medium-high heat. Add celery, onion, thyme, rosemary, sage and nutmeg. Cover; cook 3 minutes or until onion is tender. Add broth, apple juice and apple. Bring to a boil; stir in pasta. Cook, uncovered, 8 to 10 minutes.

3. Peel skin from sweet potato; cut into 1-inch pieces. Add chicken and sweet potato to soup. Reduce heat to medium; simmer 5 minutes or until chicken is cooked through and pasta is tender.

makes 4 to 6 servings

Serving Suggestion: Serve with warm herb-cheese bread.

simple soups

chicken tortellini soup

6   cups chicken broth

1   package (9 ounces) refrigerated cheese and spinach tortellini

1   package (about 6 ounces) refrigerated fully cooked chicken breast strips, cut into 1-inch pieces

2   cups baby spinach

4   to 6 tablespoons grated Parmesan cheese

1   tablespoon chopped fresh chives *or* 2 tablespoons sliced green onion

1. Bring broth to a boil in large saucepan over high heat; add tortellini. Reduce heat to medium; cook 5 minutes. Stir in chicken and spinach.

2. Reduce heat to low; cook 3 minutes or until chicken is heated through. Sprinkle with Parmesan cheese and chives.

makes 4 servings

Serving Suggestion: Make simple soup into a super supper by serving it in individual bread bowls. Purchase small, round loaves of a hearty bread, such as Italian or sourdough. Cut a small slice from the top and then remove the inside of the loaf, leaving a 1 1/2-inch shell. Pour in soup and serve.

zesty chicken & vegetable soup

½   pound boneless skinless chicken breasts, cut into very thin strips

1   to 2 tablespoons FRANK'S® REDHOT® Original Cayenne Pepper Sauce

4   cups chicken broth

1   package (16 ounces) frozen stir-fry vegetables

1   cup angel hair pasta or fine egg noodles, broken into 2-inch lengths

1   green onion, thinly sliced

COMBINE chicken and Frank's RedHot Sauce in medium bowl; set aside.

HEAT broth to boiling in large saucepan over medium-high heat. Add vegetables and pasta; return to boiling. Cook 2 minutes. Stir in chicken mixture and green onion. Cook 1 minute or until chicken is no longer pink.

makes 4 to 6 servings

Tip: For a change of pace, substitute 6 prepared frozen pot stickers for the pasta. Add to broth in step 2 and boil until tender.

recipe index

recipe index

recipe index

recipe index

acknowledgments

The publisher would like to thank the companies listed below for
the use of their recipes and photographs in this publication.

Dole Food Company, Inc.
Ortega®, A Division of B&G Foods, Inc.
Reckitt Benckiser LLC.
Unilever

metric conversion chart

VOLUME MEASUREMENTS (dry)

$^1/_8$ teaspoon = 0.5 mL
$^1/_4$ teaspoon = 1 mL
$^1/_2$ teaspoon = 2 mL
$^3/_4$ teaspoon = 4 mL
1 teaspoon = 5 mL
1 tablespoon = 15 mL
2 tablespoons = 30 mL
$^1/_4$ cup = 60 mL
$^1/_3$ cup = 75 mL
$^1/_2$ cup = 125 mL
$^2/_3$ cup = 150 mL
$^3/_4$ cup = 175 mL
1 cup = 250 mL
2 cups = 1 pint = 500 mL
3 cups = 750 mL
4 cups = 1 quart = 1 L

VOLUME MEASUREMENTS (fluid)

1 fluid ounce (2 tablespoons) = 30 mL
4 fluid ounces ($^1/_2$ cup) = 125 mL
8 fluid ounces (1 cup) = 250 mL
12 fluid ounces (1$^1/_2$ cups) = 375 mL
16 fluid ounces (2 cups) = 500 mL

WEIGHTS (mass)

$^1/_2$ ounce = 15 g
1 ounce = 30 g
3 ounces = 90 g
4 ounces = 120 g
8 ounces = 225 g
10 ounces = 285 g
12 ounces = 360 g
16 ounces = 1 pound = 450 g

DIMENSIONS

$^1/_{16}$ inch = 2 mm
$^1/_8$ inch = 3 mm
$^1/_4$ inch = 6 mm
$^1/_2$ inch = 1.5 cm
$^3/_4$ inch = 2 cm
1 inch = 2.5 cm

OVEN TEMPERATURES

250°F = 120°C
275°F = 140°C
300°F = 150°C
325°F = 160°C
350°F = 180°C
375°F = 190°C
400°F = 200°C
425°F = 220°C
450°F = 230°C

BAKING PAN AND DISH EQUIVALENTS

Utensil	Size in Inches	Size in Centimeters	Volume	Metric Volume
Baking or Cake Pan (square or rectangular)	8×8×2	20×20×5	8 cups	2 L
	9×9×2	23×23×5	10 cups	2.5 L
	13×9×2	33×23×5	12 cups	3 L
Loaf Pan	8$^1/_2$×4$^1/_2$×2$^1/_2$	21×11×6	6 cups	1.5 L
	9×9×3	23×13×7	8 cups	2 L
Round Layer Cake Pan	8×1$^1/_2$	20×4	4 cups	1 L
	9×1$^1/_2$	23×4	5 cups	1.25 L
Pie Plate	8×1$^1/_2$	20×4	4 cups	1 L
	9×1$^1/_2$	23×4	5 cups	1.25 L
Baking Dish or Casserole			1 quart/4 cups	1 L
			1$^1/_2$ quart/6 cups	1.5 L
			2 quart/8 cups	2 L
			3 quart/12 cups	3 L